The
Connell Guide
to

Anglo-Norman England
1035-1189

---

by Daniel Gerrard

Contents

NOTES

The Anglo Saxon world

The inheritance of Wessex

The pagan Viking invasions of the ninth century very nearly destroyed English civilisation, but they also created the foundations of the English state. Coming first as raiders, later as conquerors and settlers, they looted and burned their way across the English countryside. In particular, they devastated the once-thriving monastic church that preserved and propagated learning, art, and culture in the Middle Ages.

In doing so, however, they swept clean the board of high politics. Where once there had been a mosaic of Anglo-Saxon kingdoms – Wessex, Kent, Mercia, East Anglia, Northumbria, Essex and Sussex – by the end of the ninth century only Wessex remained. In consequence, the king of Wessex, Alfred the Great (who died in 899) was able to present himself as the leader of a unified Christian resistance, and even to experiment with the language of a unified nation as *Rex Angul-Saxonum* (King of the Anglo-Saxons).

Wessex, however, was a relatively compact kingdom on the English south coast. The reconquest of Viking territory that began in Alfred's reign was based on strenuous campaigning, and the building of fortified towns (*burhs*), and it demanded a remarkable effort of military and political organisation, sustained for decades. Culminating in the reigns of Alfred's successors Aethelstan (d. 939) and Edgar "the peaceable" (d. 975), England emerged as by far the most powerful polity in the British archipelago, and with approximately its modern territorial extent. English kings claimed a wider overlordship of the British Isles, even using the title *Basileus* (the title of the Byzantine emperors), and could make marriage alliances with the most powerful European monarchs. They also had perhaps the most sophisticated, systematic and intensive system of administration anywhere in the medieval west.

The new kingdom was unusual in several important respects:

1. It was organised into standard units. The Shire (which eventually came to be presided over by a royal official, the Shire-Reeve – *Sheriff*) was divided into sub-units, known as hundreds. Each hundred was composed of a number of *Hides* (a unit of agricultural production in theory approximately representing the land that could support one family or one plough team)

2. This systematic organisation allowed for the systematic use of resources. In theory, for example, one soldier could be levied from every five hides for the *fyrd* (army). A system of national taxation (itself a deeply unusual phenomenon in the period), the *Danegeld,* originally protection money used to pay off the

Vikings, was also levied on the hide.

3. The only coinage produced in England was royal. On the continent, the greater nobility often chose to mint their own coins, meaning that in many places, there were many different forms of coinage in circulation. In England, the standard coin was the silver penny. These were low-value (indicating that they were used in everyday transactions and hence that the English economy was highly-monetised), and were produced in vast quantity. They were also recoined every few years (i.e. they were collected, melted down, and remade). The king, naturally took a cut at this point.

4. English kings made national, written lawcodes. These varied a good deal in content and tone, and there has been a good deal of debate over the extent to which they were enforced, but they were an important step in developing a system of law. The codes also regulated aspects of trade, and levied lucrative fines from malefactors.

5. The English aristocracy were less territorial than their continental counterparts. Although English society was dominated by a warrior nobility whose sons could reasonably expect to occupy approximately the same social status as their fathers, they remained to some extent royal officials who could be moved, promoted, or demoted as the king wished. This prevented the

emergence of an entrenched senior nobility capable of defying royal authority.

In short, the English monarchy that emerged in the middle of the tenth century had been equipped by the struggle against the Vikings with a remarkably systematic administration capable of extracting resources in silver and men from across the nation and enacting justice in the king's name. Until recently, historians tended to believe that much of this system long predated Alfred the Great's day,[*] though George Molyneaux has challenged that position by arguing that the state apparatus only took shape in the mid tenth century[**]. Historians have, however, been consistently impressed with the administrative and technical achievements of the late Anglo-Saxon state. Nevertheless, the Anglo-Saxon state was successfully invaded and conquered not once, but twice in the course of the 11th century.

Cnut and the Conquest of 1016-17

The name of King Aethelred "the Unready" (d 1016) is associated almost exclusively with crime,

[*] The most significant exponent of what he called the "Maximum view" of the Old English state, emphasising both its achievements and its antiquity was James Campbell. See his essays collected in *The Anglo-Saxon State* (2000).
[**] See G. Molyneaux, "Why were some tenth century English kings presented as rulers of Britain?" in *Transactions of the Royal Historical Society* 21 (2011), pp. 59-91 and *The Formation of the English Kingdom in the Tenth Century* (2015)

chaos and catastrophe, but this is somewhat unfair. The king could neither have predicted nor prevented the renewal of large-scale Viking attacks led by Danish kings on England in his reign. He responded sensibly to the crisis by marrying Emma, the daughter of Duke Richard of Normandy, creating a marriage alliance that denied the Vikings use of Normandy's ports for their attacks.

The famous English defeat at the Battle of Maldon (991) did not lead to political collapse. Indeed, Aethelred fought the Vikings for more than 20 years, and his eventual defeat may owe as much to political division as military difficulties; both sides saw repeated defections in this period, but the defections of Ealdorman Eadric Streona of Mercia and Earl Uhtred of East Anglia to the Danes were probably the most significant. When Aethelred died in 1016, he was succeeded by his son, Edmund "Ironside", who suffered a major defeat by the Danes at Ashingdon, leading to a temporary division of the kingdom. When Edmund died, the Danish prince, Cnut, finally succeeded him unopposed.

The Danish conquest had taken a whole generation, and was hardly conclusive. Cnut came to the throne of a country exhausted by war as much because he survived Edmund Ironside as a result of military victories. It should be little surprise that he tried to present himself not as a foreign conqueror, but as an English king. His first political act was to wed Aethelred's widow, Emma. The leaders of the English church were left in place, and supported the new regime with their authority and expertise. Though extensive lands were given to Cnut's Danish followers, the Anglo-Saxon aristocracy was not wholly disinherited. Crucially, as ruler of Denmark, Cnut could offer the English guaranteed protection against renewed violence from across the North Sea, a promise made more certain when he added Norway to his holdings in 1028.

Though Cnut was keen to present himself as the candidate of continuity, he oversaw a quiet revolution in the structure of the English state that would have long-term consequences. He simply could not supervise the whole of his widespread dominions in person. His solution was to impose a new layer of government in England, carving the country into four large Earldoms (Wessex, Mercia, Northumbria and East Anglia) with substantial autonomy. Wessex, the heartland of the Anglo-Saxon monarchy, was entrusted to a man of obscure background called Godwine.

Cnut's system worked as long as the king lived. His prestige, the loyalty of the earls, and the substantial resources he could draw on as an international ruler kept England under control, but in November 1035 he died and his legacy began to unravel.

Harold I, Harthacnut, and Edward "the Confessor"

The politics of the period 1035-1042 are deeply obscure, but the key points are these: in 1035, Cnut was succeeded by Harold I ("Harefoot"), probably because his brother Harthacnut was in Denmark and unable to press his claim. Alfred, an exiled son of Aethelred II, attempted to launch an invasion of England from Normandy, but was betrayed by Earl Godwine of Wessex and murdered. When Harold died in 1040, he was succeeded by his brother Harthacnut, who like Cnut combined the kingship in England with that of Denmark. He summoned his half-brother Edward back from Normandy. The new king's prospects looked good, but he too died suddenly in 1042.

Edward (later known as "the Confessor") had a position in English politics quite unlike that of any previous king. Although he was unquestionably the legitimate heir of the ancient Wessex monarchy, he was in some respects an alien in his own country. During the reigns of Cnut and Harold Harefoot, Edward had lived in exile with his mother's family in Normandy.

The youth of medieval kings was an important period, the time when they established a loyal network of followers. As an exile, Edward effectively skipped this period, coming to his throne with no following and no military reputation. He was unmarried, childless and middle-aged.

To his great misfortune, he also inherited the political structure of four great earldoms established by Cnut and maintained by Harthacnut. Unlike Cnut, however, Edward had neither the military prestige, nor the ability to draw on armies raised in

England in 1066, showing the most significant regions and cities, and the most important battlefields.

Scandinavia, to buttress his position. Even in retrospect, it is difficult to see what he could have done to match the rising power of Earl Godwine of Wessex.

Godwine understood his opportunity perfectly well. In 1045, Edward married Godwine's daughter Edith. In two generations, Godwine's family had gone from obscurity to alliance with one of Europe's most ancient royal houses! How enthusiastic Edward was to marry the daughter of an overmighty earl who had murdered his brother, Alfred, cannot be known, but can perhaps be guessed. In truth, we know nothing about Edward and Edith's domestic arrangements except that Godwine's evident ambition that he should be the grandfather of kings was not to be fulfilled. It is the central fact of Edward's political life that he and Edith produced no children.

The crisis of Edward's reign began in 1051. Although he had little room for manoeuvre in secular politics, one undoubted royal prerogative was the appointment of bishops. Unsurprisingly, Edward chose a Norman, Robert of Jumièges, for the key position of Archbishop of Canterbury. In doing so, he blocked the advancement of Abbot Aethelric, Godwine's favoured candidate for the post.

Shortly afterwards, a fight broke out at Dover between some of Godwine's followers and those of Count Eustace of Boulogne, one of Edward's relatives and allies. The country appeared to be sliding toward civil war, and Godwine and the king both raised armies. Surprisingly, though, Godwine's position suddenly collapsed. Earls Leofric and Siward, when finally pressed by military crisis, chose to support the king, and, according to the *Anglo-Saxon Chronicle,* Godwine's troops refused to fight fellow Englishmen. Godwine and his sons fled into exile.

Edward's period as the master of England was brief and of little lasting consequence, but we can perhaps glimpse a faint outline of what might have been. Edith was bundled off to a convent. A reissue of the coinage showed Edward apparently in military mood, wearing a helmet. In any event, Godwine and his sons returned from exile with two new armies in 1052. London defected to the earl and the king's power collapsed as swiftly as Godwine's had the previous year.

In theory, there was then a reconciliation between king and earl. In practice, the crisis seems to have broken whatever power remained to Edward. After 1052 he is hardly mentioned in the *Anglo-Saxon Chronicle,* and Edith returned to court. Robert of Jumièges was exiled for causing discord, and the archbishopric passed to Stigand.

Godwine's death in 1053 did nothing to revive Edward's independent rule. Instead, Godwine's son Harold took over his father's position and cemented it. In the next five years, no fewer than three of Harold's brothers received earldoms. The power of Earls Leofric and Siward was eclipsed and England became something very like a family firm. Harold won stunning military victories over the Welsh in the 1050s, and was sufficiently secure in his position to be able to travel outside the kingdom, visiting Rome, Flanders and Germany. The only real failure of his power came in 1065 when a rebellion broke out in the north over the misrule of his younger brother, Earl Tostig, but Tostig was forced into exile and order soon restored.

At the end of 1065, Harold's position seemed solid, his domination of English politics apparently unassailable, and the future of Godwine's dynasty secure. The government of England, however, still continued to be conducted in the name of King Edward, the heir of the ancient Wessex dynasty. On

4th or 5th January 1066, however, the King died and Anglo-Saxon England came crashing down.

France and the Dukes of Normandy

Across the Channel lay a polity of quite different type and history. Where the development of the English monarchy can be thought of as an evolutionary response to Viking pressure, that same pressure had accelerated the breakdown of the French monarchy in the tenth century, encouraging the development of an independent aristocracy whose power was based on castles.

The duchy of Normandy (the land of the Northmen) was founded as a Viking territory in northern France. The first Norman duke, Rollo, had carved the territory out of the lands of a feeble French monarchy in the mid tenth century. There are no signs of hostility between Normandy and England before 1066. Aethelred's alliance had proved durable, and Norman merchants enjoyed privileges in English law.

The Latin word *dux* (the origin of the French *duc* and the English *duke*) originally meant "general", and the Normans enjoyed a formidable reputation as warriors. Although vassals of the French king, the dukes were for the most part functionally independent rulers. In practice, the kings of France controlled a relatively small (though rich) slice of territory between Paris and Orlèans. To the west and south, the counts of Anjou had emerged as a comparable force to the dukes of Normandy. The county of Maine had the misfortune of being caught between its more powerful Norman and Angevin neighbours.

As David Bates has pointed out, much of the history of France in the mid 11th century is the story of the struggle for supremacy between those three powers – Normandy, Anjou, and France.* When one of the three seemed to be on the verge of achieving pre-eminence, it would be checked by an alliance of the other two. While that balance of power guaranteed perpetual struggle, it also gave all three an interest in each other's survival.

The most striking example of this came in 1042 at the Battle of Val-ès Dunes. After a long period of disorder during the childhood of the young Duke William of Normandy, in which major rebellions by the nobility of the duchy had seriously disrupted the ducal government, William was beginning to reassert his dominance. How severe that disorder was is a matter of debate. The leading historian of the Conqueror, David Bates, argues that it was less pronounced than was once thought. Even so, it was doubtless substantial. Much of the credit for William's victory at his first major battle, however, probably belongs to the intervention there of an army commanded by the King of France, Henri I.

Duke William was a ruler of a very different sort from Edward the Confessor. He was heir to neither

---

* David Bates, *William the Conqueror* (1989)

a strong administrative tradition nor the cosmic dignity of kingship. He had, however, spent his young life forging a reputation for military success and ruthlessness, and building the network of close comrades which would later form a key component of his rule. He was also more fortunate in his marriage than Edward, wedding Mathilda, daughter of the Count of Flanders in about 1050. This brought him children and an alliance with one of the other major powers in the region. It also seems to have brought him a happy and loving marriage with a highly capable woman who could play an important political role when required.

In short, England and Normandy were profoundly different polities in 1066. One was the hegemonic power in the British Isles with a remarkable and robust administrative system, but whose recent rulers had been hobbled by invasion, dynastic failure and political weakness. The other was smaller, poorer, and existed in tension with two other small powers of comparable strength. It lacked a developed administrative tradition, but its ruler had emerged from a period of political and military turmoil with a reputation for ruthless military prowess. The coming conflict between the two would have profound effects on the British Isles and on north-western Europe more generally for centuries to come.

The Norman Conquest of England (1066-1070)

A short summary of what happened

Harold moved quickly to take the crown. Archbishop Stigand performed the coronation at Westminster Abbey immediately, and there seems to have been no domestic opposition to his accession. Duke William also decided to press a claim to the English throne, but that would require an invasion conducted on a massive scale.

Though called a "Norman" invasion by historians, the campaign of 1066 was not conducted exclusively by Norman forces. William recruited warriors from across northern France. Pope Alexander II was persuaded to endorse the invasion (and indeed sent a special banner for William's army to carry into battle). Meanwhile, construction of the navy that would carry his army across the English Channel began in earnest.

William's furious diplomatic and logistical preparations for the invasion could hardly be missed, and Harold took appropriate measures to defend his position against the coming invasion. The English army was summoned and spread out along the south coast to hinder any landing by Norman forces. Harold himself made his base of operations on the Isle of Wight, and there he waited. And waited.

However impressive William's preparations, it was simply impossible for him to cross the Channel without favourable weather, but the wind refused to cooperate. He and his army were forced to remain at St Valery. As autumn approached, Harold may have decided that it was now too late in the year for William to begin a campaign and dismissed much of his army. In any event, much of the English army was composed of peasant levies who could not be kept under arms indefinitely; they needed to return home to gather the harvest. For the moment, the crisis seemed to have passed. Then Harold received what must have been shattering news. The King of Norway, Harald Hardraada, had allied with Harold's exiled brother, Earl Tostig, and had invaded Yorkshire.

A former leader of the Byzantine Emperor's "Varangian" Guard, Harald Hardraada enjoyed one of the most impressive military reputations of any contemporary warrior. His sudden appearance in the north of England with a large army (the *Anglo-Saxon Chronicle* suggested that it came borne by a fleet of 300 ships), was as much a threat to the existence of Harold's kingship as any of Duke William's plans. Picking up reinforcements from Shetland and Orkney, Hardraada reached the mouth of the Tyne on about 10th September 1066. On 20th September, he was met by the forces of the two northern earls, Edwin and Morcar. Hardraada smashed them at the Battle of Fulford. On 24th September, the city of York surrendered, and he set about consolidating his hold on the region.

King Harold's response to this new threat was decisive. Reassembling his army at breakneck speed, he drove north in a remarkable forced march to catch the Norwegians before they could penetrate any further into England. Hardraada was waiting at Stamford Bridge for the surrender of local hostages that would have guaranteed his position in the north when Harold's army suddenly attacked him there. The Battle of Stamford Bridge was an extraordinarily brutal and bloody affair, but at the end of the day Hardraada and Tostig were both dead and only a tiny remnant of their army was allowed to slip back to Norway.

Harold's achievement should not be underestimated. Though he could not know it, he had won the last great battle ever to be fought between Viking invaders and an English royal army. He had no time to savour his victory, however, and we can only guess at his reaction when he learned that the wind had finally turned and that Duke William's invasion of England had begun.

William's army crossed the Channel overnight from 27th-28th September 1066 and landed at Pevensey before dawn. They quickly established a temporary fortress and began to terrorise the south coast, ravaging the region to demonstrate that King Harold could not fulfil the primary function of kingship: the protection of his subjects. Harold immediately began a second rapid march across the length of England, blocking William's route to

London, and took up a defensive position on Senlac Hill. William's army attacked him there on 14th October 1066.

Most medieval battles were quite short affairs. The Battle of Hastings was not. Neither army could afford to lose. For the invaders, defeat would mean being trapped on the wrong side of the Channel in a hostile land, with winter approaching. For the English, defeat would mean that the road to London, and with it, victory, was open to the Normans. The result was a long, bloody battle of attrition that took all day, and was a very close-run thing. Though the English seem to have lacked the archers and cavalry that were an important part of the Norman army, they had the advantage of a strong defensive position, and the Norman army might well have shattered itself trying to attack them.

At one point, it appeared that William himself had been killed, and his army began to rout. English soldiers began to stream down the hill to chase the Normans from the field. The situation was apparently saved by the quick intervention of Bishop Odo of Bayeux, the duke's half-brother, and by a dramatic gesture on William's part, throwing off his helmet to show his men that he still lived. William was able to rally his fleeing troops, who turned back on their pursuers and cut them down, a testimony not only to his charismatic leadership but to the remarkable training and discipline of Norman cavalry.

Opposite: Portrait of William the Conqueror (c.1620)

The English position was weakened by these losses, and may have been weakened yet further by a series of apparent withdrawals designed to tempt English soldiers into abandoning their position to give chase. Eventually, the cohesion of the English army began to break down. Harold himself fell, as did his two surviving brothers, Gyrth and Leofwine.

William had won a decisive victory, but that was not yet the same as securing control of the kingdom. London still presented a serious obstacle. The surviving English leadership (including Archbishop Stigand) rallied there, putting forward Edgar "Aetheling" as king.* Edgar was a 14-year-old great-nephew of Edward the Confessor.

Rather than advancing straight on the city, where a single narrow bridge crossed the Thames, and where his powerful cavalry and archery would be less decisive, William first secured a series of important strategic towns in the south of England: Dover, Canterbury, and Winchester. In doing so, he isolated the city before advancing from a secure position. In early December, Edgar submitted to William at Berkhamstead. William was crowned at Westminster Abbey by Archbishop Ealdred of York on Christmas day 1066.

Over the next few years, his rule was challenged by a series of English revolts. These were all based in areas that were physically remote from the

* "Aetheling" was used by the Anglo-Saxons to designate the heir-apparent to the throne. After the Norman Conquest, this was rendered "Adelin".

centres of power in the south, or were in regions where the terrain made counter-insurgency operations difficult. None were successful.

Hereward "the wake" based himself at the monastery of Ely and ran a guerrilla campaign from the fens. Edric "the wild" made common cause with the Welsh to ravage the area around Hereford. In 1068, the citizens of Exeter seem to have emerged at the head of a brief coalition of south-western rebel towns, an interesting and very early case of an urban revolt.

The only insurgency really to threaten the regime, however, took place in Northumbria. Early in 1069, Northumbrian rebels under the command of Edgar Aetheling entered the city of York. The northern rebels received the support of King Swein of Denmark, and in 1070 it appeared that a full Danish invasion of the north was imminent. William, however, reached an agreement with Swein before this could materialise.

All of these revolts were crushed by William's army. But the gravity of the northern revolt is indicated by the severity of William's response to it. While Edgar fled to Scotland, he began a massive campaign of reprisal, known as "The Harrying of the North", devastating the region with fire and sword. Military campaigns of this period were often brutal, but the destruction of much of northern England was regarded as unusually harsh, even by contemporaries.

Why was there a succession crisis in 1066?

The dynastic politics of 11th century Europe were personal, bitter, and ferocious. Crises, and indeed civil wars, were perfectly normal when kings died. The principal reason for this is that the conventions by which kings succeeded had not yet hardened into fixed rules and no institution existed that could police them. That said, the position of England's ruling dynasty when Edward the Confessor died was unusually fragile. Edgar Aetheling was no match for seasoned warriors like William, Harold, or Harald Hardraada.

It should also be remembered that all of the other claimants could make substantial arguments in favour of their own legitimacy to succeed:

1. Harald Hardraada could claim that as King of Denmark he had a right to the English monarchy as a restoration of Cnut's empire.

2. Harold claimed (entirely plausibly) that Edward had entrusted the kingdom to him on his deathbed.

3. William claimed that Harold had become his vassal during a visit to Normandy in 1064. As such, this promise predated Edward's deathbed bequest, and so was the stronger claim. He could also claim closer kinship to Edward through

Edward's mother, Emma of Normandy, who had been the daughter of his great grandfather, Duke Richard I. William also claimed that Harold's consecration at the hands of the corrupt Stigand was uncanonical (i.e. illegal under the conventions of the "canon" law of the church) and therefore invalid.

Within this dispute, there was one cardinal fact: Edward the Confessor died childless, leaving behind great uncertainty over the succession. In the immediate aftermath of 1066, this could be easily explained by claiming that Edward refrained from sex as an act of personal piety. This claim, advanced by the *Life of King Edward Who Rests at Westminster* is the origin of the notion that Edward was a saint.

Modern historians are unconvinced, and disagree on the question of whether Edward bears some responsibility for the events that followed his death. Frank Barlow sees Edward as a sharp political operator who dangled the promise of succession before multiple possible claimants to keep potential rivals off balance and compensate for the structural weaknesses of his government.[*] Stephen Baxter, on the other hand, has argued that Edward's failure to address the succession issue decisively was a terrible political failure, and that the king bears substantial

---

[*] F. Barlow, *Edward the Confessor* (1970, 1979)

responsibility for all that followed.*

Why was the Norman invasion successful?

The Norman Conquest was a dramatic success. In a few short months, it made the ruler of one polity into the master of another. In a few short years, it made his government effective across the whole country and made the prospect of large-scale native revolt impossible.

This sort of decisive conquest conducted in a single campaign was most unusual in the high middle ages, the best contemporary comparison probably being the staggering military successes of the First Crusade (1095-99), a risky, but wildly successful campaign which swiftly established new polities on the eastern coast of the Mediterranean.

The Norman Conquest stands in marked contrast to the slower and more partial Danish invasions of 1016-17. It also stands in marked contrast to William the Conqueror's other campaigns. Though widely regarded as an effective warrior, he repeatedly tried to reduce the tiny French county of Maine to obedience – a process far from complete by his death. This, it must be said, was the normal pattern of western European warfare in the period. Campaigning adjusted borders or

* S. Baxter, "Edward the Confessor and the succession question" in (ed.) R. Mortimer, *Edward the Confessor: The man and the legend* (2009), pp. 77-118

modified the relative status of rulers. It did not usually destroy a whole political organism. We must therefore turn our attention to the question of why the Norman Conquest was so successful.

Long-term factors

Some historians look to the Norman Conquest as the culmination of long-term processes or even of wider European trends. There are four main manifestations of this approach:

1. Decline and fall: Some historians (notably Richard Abels) advance the view that the Norman Conquest was made possible by a long-term decline in the effectiveness of English military institutions.[*] Though this approach has the virtue of explaining both the Danish and the Norman Conquests, it is unconvincing because no contemporary wrote that English arms were in decline. Nor does it take into account Harold II's decisive defeat of Harald Hardraada.

2. Norman exceptionalism: Some historians (notably David Douglas) observe that England was far from the only forum in which the Normans won substantial military victories in this period.[**] Norman exiles and crusaders car-

[*]   R. Abels "The Military Failure of the Late Anglo-Saxon State" in R. Abels, B. Bachrach (eds.) *The Normans and their Adversaries at War: Essays in Honour of C. Warren Hollister* (2001)
[**]   D. Douglas, *The Norman Achievement (1050-1150)* (1969)

ved out new kingdoms for themselves in Sicily/ Southern Italy and the Eastern Mediterranean in the 11th and 12th centuries. The superiority of Norman warriors over their contemporaries is an attractive explanation, and certainly one the Normans themselves believed, though it does not help us with the problem of why William was so unsuccessful in his attempts to conquer Maine.

3. The expansion of Europe: Some historians (notably Robert Bartlett) understand the wider sweep of European history in the period 900-1300 as turning on "expansion".* They observe that there was a clear cultural, technological, religious and political similarity between the polities in a zone roughly matching the old Carolingian Empire, and that these countries used a form of warfare based on castles and heavy cavalry (knights) to conduct successful conquests on every frontier of that zone – the Normans conquered England (and then moved into Scotland, Wales, and Ireland). The kingdoms of Christian Iberia successfully "reconquered" most of the rest of the peninsula. Other groups of Normans established kingdoms in the central and Eastern Mediterranean. Crusades captured substantial territory in the Eastern Mediterranean and the Baltic.

* R. Bartlett, *The Making of Europe: Conquest, colonization and cultural change: 950-1350* (1993)

The great advantage of this explanation is that it encourages us to think more widely about European history rather than concentrating narrowly on England and France. It may also encourage us, though, to think of Anglo-Saxon England as more different from the Continent than was really the case. The artists of the Bayeux Tapestry, for instance, make very clear that the arms and armour of English warriors at the Battle of Hastings were, to all intents and purposes, identical to those of the invaders.

4. Castles: It is often remarked that the Normans were largely responsible for the introduction of castles into England. This formidable new military technology was certainly key to consolidating Norman rule, but it may also help explain why William was so much more successful in England than in Maine. His campaigns in Maine largely revolved around the slow reduction of fortifications. In England, his armies were able to move much more freely. Since the lack of castles in England can be thought of as expressive of the central power of the late Anglo-Saxon state, it may be the case that the Norman Conquest was successful as much because of England's powerful state as in spite of it.

Short-term factors

The Normans' success was also affected by short-term factors, the most important of which was timing.

1. The need to defeat Harald Hardraada in the north created major problems for Harold II. His army marched most of the length of England twice in the autumn of 1066 and must have arrived at Senlac Hill disorganised and exhausted. By all accounts, the Battles of Fulford and Stanford Bridge had inflicted horrible casualties on the English. In short, Harold brought to the Battle of Hastings a tired army that was about to start its third major engagement of the campaign. William's, in contrast, was rested, fresh and intact.

2. It should also be remembered that Norman dukes were not normally able to leave their duchies for long periods; the need to be ready to defend or intervene against the count of Anjou or the king of France was ever-present. By chance, however, the king in 1066 (Philip I) was a child, while the count of Anjou (Geoffrey III) was an incompetent, distracted by a conflict brewing with his brother. The Norman Conquest took place in a very narrow chronological window during which William could afford to turn his attention away from northern France and towards England.

Three other short-term factors are worth mentioning:

1. Diplomacy: William's forces were bolstered by warriors from across northern France, and encouraged by the authority of the papacy, manifested in a banner that they carried into battle.

2. Luck: William seems to have been nearly killed at least once during the Battle of Hastings. His rival was actually killed. That situation could easily have been reversed.

3. Terror: Even in the brutal context of 11th century warfare, the harrying of the north was regarded as unusually ferocious. The Battle of Hastings had eliminated a large part of the English nobility, while savage ravaging of the countryside and the erection of new castles in important strategic sites (including every major town) made abundantly clear that the penalties for defiance were likely to be severe. After 1070, there were few left who would take the risk.

What were the effects of the Norman Conquest?

There is no settled consensus about this. Some historians emphasise continuity after 1066; others see the period as marking a sharp break which profoundly and permanently affected the development of the country.

For the peasantry, the effect of the conquest depended largely on geography. In parts of northern England, the effect was truly catastrophic, bringing physical devastation that was clearly visible decades later. Large areas of many towns were demolished to make way for urban castles. The damage inflicted on the peasantry is clear from declining land values and increased "waste" – both described in the Domesday Book (1086).

In other areas of Britain, the rural economy (and presumably the condition of the peasantry) had improved a good deal by the end of the 11th century. But even in these areas improvements were uneven: while the slave trade was prohibited in England in 1102, and slavery vanished quite quickly in the generation or two following the Conquest, the Normans seem to have been much more aggressive in exploiting labour, perhaps reducing the distinction between slaves and free peasants.

The effect of the conquest on the English nobility is much more clear-cut. It was sudden and disastrous. A large proportion of the nobles were killed in the battles of 1066. Others fled into exile, many of them joining the Emperor of Byzantium's Varangian Guard. Those who remained found most of their lands taken from them to reward William's followers.

Women in the nobility also paid a heavy price, perhaps an even heavier price than the men. Some noble women benefited from marriage to incoming Normans; others, though, who owned their own land, had a tougher time. The Normans placed much more emphasis on the the importance of landholders performing military duties than the Anglo-Saxons had – putting women landowners at a disadvantage. On the other hand, the reforms to the English Church that took place after 1066 included changes to the concept of marriage. Archbishop Lanfranc, in particular, was a key figure in advancing the view that marriage required the consent of the woman to be valid.

The effect on culture

It is possible to see the Norman Conquest as a cultural disaster. Before 1066, England was the only country in western Europe whose administrators used the vernacular (rather than Latin). English also had a grand tradition of vernacular literature, especially in verse. This tradition was largely severed by the arrival of a new elite whose main spoken language was Norman French, and whose main administrative language was Latin.

Although the tradition of *Beowulf* disappeared relatively quickly, some of the best Norman French literature was produced in Anglo-Norman England. The tradition of the *Chanson de Roland,* and eventually of King Arthur, rose to take the place of Anglo-Saxon heroic poetry. The early 12th century also saw a remarkable flowering of Latin historical writing, much of it produced in monasteries, the main spur of which may have been the need to understand the role of divine providence in bringing the conquest to pass and to understand the place of monasteries in the new regime.

Meanwhile, the arrival of a French-speaking aristocracy profoundly influenced the development of English by injecting a huge number of French and Latin words into the English lexicon. When English emerged again as a literary language in the late 13th and 14th centuries, it did so greatly enriched by this influence.

The same can be said about art and architecture. Relatively little of this survives from late Anglo-Saxon England, and the conquerors certainly tore down many Anglo-Saxon churches. What arose in the place of these old buildings, however, was a remarkable number of new ones executed in English variations of the continental "Romanesque" style, some of which still survive.

The church after 1066

The mid 11th century saw profound changes sweep through the wider European Church. Known as "Papal Reform" or "Gregorian Reform", this movement sought to purify the church by making it more independent from secular power, improving the standard of observance in monasteries, cracking down on the purchase of church offices (Simony) and on clerical marriage, and increasing the power of the papacy.

England was already being affected by these

changes before 1066, but the Norman Conquest pulled England more firmly into the mainstream of Papal Reform. The papal agenda provided the excuse to remove most of England's senior clergy from their posts around 1070 and replace them with appointees from the continent. There was short-term looting of English churches and some damage to their property, but the institutions came through the conquest largely intact, and many of them were rebuilt in the years that followed.

The consequences of the Norman Conquest for England have been much debated. Historians have given far less attention to the consequences for France, though these were significant too. The Duke of Normandy was already a major player in north-ern French politics; by 1070 he was a monarch in his own right, with the resources of a large and well-organised kingdom to draw upon. The first occasion on which English troops are recorded as being used to fight the King-Duke's wars in France was as early as 1073. English kings would continue to control important lands in France until 1558, a situation that disrupted the development of the French monarchy and almost guaranteed a series of wars between the two kingdoms that lasted for the rest of the middle ages.

FIVE FACTS ABOUT
ENGLAND, 1035-1189

1. The most famous medieval mythology – the stories of King Arthur – began to take shape in this period. *The History of the Kings of Britain*, by Geoffrey of Monmouth, was a wildly popular work which was mistaken for a reliable account of early medieval Britain for centuries after its composition c. 1135.

2. Although a deeply hierarchical and religiously conservative society, there was a healthy appetite for scandalous gossip about the powerful in England in this period and no formal system of state censorship. For example, it was rumoured that Eleanor of Aquitaine found time during the Second Crusade to have an affair with her own uncle, Raymond of Antioch!

3. The story that Harold II was killed by an arrow in the eye is an early one. It is found in early 12th century accounts of the Battle of Hastings and may even be illustrated in The

Bayeux Tapestry. Unfortunately, the caption in the Tapestry, *Hic Haroldus Rex Interfectus Est* (Here King Harold is killed), runs above the heads of two figures, one being cut down by a Norman horseman, and another with an arrow protruding from the eye. It is unclear whether Harold is represented by one or both of these figures.

4. William the Conqueror banned the slave trade in England, apparently with great success. Within 20 years of his arrival, the number of slaves in the kingdom was already in steep decline. By the early 12th century, slavery had vanished completely.

5. Although the great majority of the population was committed to agriculture, the English economy made use of substantial technology and infrastructure. The great salt works at Droitwich consumed large quantities of wood as fuel, and by 1086 England already had some 6,000 water mills installed.

The English state (1070-1135)

There was no realistic possibility of an Anglo-Saxon revival, but that did not mean that there was a shortage of enemies left for William to fight, and the period after 1070 was anything but stable. We can divide the most important developments into three areas: the struggle for control of the Anglo-Norman *Regnum* within William the Conqueror's family, the difficult relationship between English kings and the church, and the continued development of the English state apparatus.

The struggle for control

William's rule after 1070 was a difficult one. He spent most of his reign across the Channel, trying to navigate the complicated currents of northern French politics and warfare. The narrow window in which Normandy was relatively secure from attack – a window that had opened just in time for Edward the Confessor's death – soon snapped shut again.

William failed to prevent the succession to the County of Flanders of Robert the Frisian, which transformed Flanders from one of his most powerful allies into a dangerous enemy. He was able to restore his authority in Maine in 1073, but faced an increasingly hostile array of forces. The power of France was reviving. So was the power of Anjou.

Worse still, the first major rebellion by William's own followers, the "revolt of the three earls", rocked the regime in 1075. William then suffered the first serious defeat of his career at the siege of Dol in 1076. His own son, Robert, frustrated by his father's refusal to give him more autonomy, allied himself with France and wounded his father in battle.

In 1082, William arrested and imprisoned his half-brother, Bishop Odo of Bayeux, apparently for treason. In 1083, his wife, Queen Matilda, died, and in 1084 Robert seems to have sought support for a second rebellion. In 1085, William anticipated another Danish invasion of England. He ravaged the east coast to make a landing more difficult and undertook the great survey of England's resources known as the Domesday Book, probably to help prepare for the coming struggle.

The invasion was only prevented by the sudden murder of the Danish king, Cnut IV. William then seems to have decided to seize the military initiative himself, launching an attack on the French town of Mantes. There he was injured; six weeks later, on 9th September 1087, he died.

The magnates assembled around William the Conqueror's deathbed fled the scene, believing that the death of the King-Duke would bring about a profound political crisis. They were quite right. The Conqueror's death began a long struggle between his three children over who would control their father's lands.

Under Norman custom, the eldest son generally

inherited the "patrimonial" lands, while a man's own conquests were divided between his other children. William's first son, Robert "Curthose", thus became Duke of Normandy, while his second son, William Rufus, became King of England. His third son, Henry, received a very large cash bequest, which he used to establish himself in western Normandy.

It was hardly surprising, however, that this situation did not last. The Conqueror's greatest followers held lands on both sides of the Channel, and it was very much in their interest that they should have a single ruler, rather than two who might come into conflict. War between Robert and Rufus broke out almost immediately, but by 1089, Rufus had seen off Robert's challenge and had acquired a secure grip on England.

Robert was an energetic campaigner, but a lethargic ruler who swiftly made himself unpopular with the Norman aristocracy and spent far beyond his means. In 1096, he decided to join the forces of the First Crusade, pawned the duchy of Normandy to Rufus and left for the Mediterranean. It seems likely that he was not expected to return.

Rufus was killed in a hunting accident in the New Forest in 1100. His younger brother, Henry, was on the spot and moved quickly to secure the royal treasure and the support of the church. He was crowned king, but his claim to the throne was very weak. He was neither a conqueror nor the eldest surviving son. He shored up his claim by issuing a "coronation charter", a statement of promises for good government and by marrying Edith/Matilda, a Scottish princess descended from the Wessex dynasty.*

Robert returned home one of the most celebrated warriors in Christendom and resumed his rule over Normandy, with the authority which that implied. While he sought again to reunite the Anglo-Norman lands through conquest, however, he was no more successful against Henry I than he had been against William Rufus. He was finally defeated and captured by Henry at the Battle of Tinchebrai in 1106. Henry had rebuilt his father's legacy, but Robert remained dangerous. He was imprisoned first at Bristol, and then at Cardiff Castle, where he remained until his death in 1134.

The reign of Henry I after 1106 brought England 30 years of relative peace. But in northern France this was a period of intense diplomatic and military activity. Normandy had to be defended against the interference of the king of France, the power of a resurgent Anjou, and the threat of Robert Curthose's eldest son, William Clito. Henry handled these threats with skill and by 1121 seemed to have built a diplomatic settlement that would hold the various

* Many English men and women of this period found themselves in a world where once normal or even fashionable English names were suddenly considered uncouth. Edith took the name Matilda for this reason. The most famous example of this trend is the English monk Orderic, who entered the Norman monastery of Saint-Evroul as a child. Finding that his name led to bullying by other novices, he adopted the more "refined" sounding "Vitalis".

powers in balance. He made his only legitimate son, William "Adelin", Duke of Normandy.

William did homage for the duchy to the king of France, and was also married to Matilda of Anjou. The long-disputed county of Maine came to him as her dowry. The young William had a high reputation. He was well-educated, a fine warrior, and the lynchpin of Henry's new diplomatic system. William and many sons of the Anglo-Norman nobility were celebrating the king's triumph on board a "White Ship" during a Channel crossing when the worst happened – the ship was wrecked, killing William, his companions and almost the entire crew.

The "White Ship Disaster" is certainly the most significant shipwreck in English history. With it collapsed not only Henry's carefully-constructed diplomatic settlement, but also his hopes for the succession. Though the king had other children – his sexual appetite seems to have been voracious – he had no other legitimate sons. A generation earlier, this would not have been a problem. William the Conqueror had been a bastard in more ways than one, but the Papal Reform's elevation of the sacrament of marriage had made the succession to the crown of an illegitimate son impossible by the middle of the 12th-century.

As Henry's plans unravelled, the king of France sought to use William Clito to destabilise Henry's rule. Clito was given lands on the Norman frontier from which to cause trouble. In 1127, King Louis VI put pressure on the Flemings to accept Clito as their new count. War was inevitable, and the crisis only came to an end when Clito was killed during an attack on the (Norman) Castle of Aast.

By 1127, it was clear that Henry was not going to produce another legitimate son. The king was fast running out of options to secure the future of his dynasty. His solution was a desperate one. Though lacking a legitimate son, he did have a legitimate daughter, Maud. She was the wife of the German Emperor Henry V and had been widowed in 1125, though still favoured the title "Empress". Henry married her again, to Count Geoffrey of Anjou, and extracted a promise from his nobles that they would support Maud's claim to both England and Normandy after his death.

The marriage alliance with Geoffrey of Anjou was a desperate move. Designed to ensure that his own descendants continued to rule England and Normandy and to neutralise the possibility of an Angevin challenge to that dynasty by joining the two families together, it was perhaps Henry's only possible move after the White Ship Disaster. His solution, however, required the testosterone-driven Anglo-Norman nobility to accept the rule of a woman, and one married to their traditional Angevin enemy. While the old king lived, his formidable authority could keep the Anglo-Norman nobility apparently united behind the plan. But on his death in 1135 it evaporated immediately.

Kings and archbishops

As the battle for control of the world created by the Norman Conquest unfolded, a second struggle developed. Less violent, but no less significant in the long-term, was the struggle for supremacy in the English church. This consisted of two strands: the debate over the relative status of England's two archbishops (at Canterbury and York), and the debate over whether the ultimate authority in ecclesiastical affairs belonged with the king, or with the pope. For our purposes, the second of these is the more important.

William the Conqueror was a sincerely pious man. No contradiction existed between piety and conquest in this period. The God that William worshipped provided victory in battle to the righteous, and William's eldest son became one of the heroes of the First Crusade. William gave thanks to God for his various favours with a series of pious benefactions including the construction of a new monastery on the site of his great victory over Harold II, at Battle.

One aspect of that piety was that William took seriously the demands of the Papal Reform movement. The papacy supported him in his struggles within Normandy in the 1050s and sent him a banner to carry into battle in 1066. Afterwards, a papal legate, Ermenfrid of Sion, helpfully provided a schedule of penance that the Norman warriors could perform to rid themselves of the moral stains incurred in fighting. But while William paid what he saw as appropriate honour to the papacy, that was a very different matter from accepting the interference of Rome in the business of his realm.

William had a powerful ally in the person of Archbishop Lanfranc of Canterbury. An Italian by birth, Lanfranc had been William's adviser and friend long before the Norman Conquest, and he was installed as Archbishop when Stigand was deposed from office in 1070.

Lanfranc was one of the foremost legal scholars in Christendom. He had played a key role in suppressing the heresy of Berengar of Tours and held a series of important councils for the furtherance of church reform. Like William, however, he believed firmly in the authority of kingship. Indeed, he played an important role in the suppression of the revolt of 1075. He also supported William in his resistance to the growing tentacles of the papacy. Lanfranc's letters to Pope Gregory VII reveal a steadily-deteriorating relationship as the pope's demands that Lanfranc come to Rome became more strident.

Lanfranc did not long outlive William the Conqueror, but he did survive long enough to throw his substantial authority behind the succession of William Rufus. This meant helping the king to handle the complicated legal business of dealing with Bishop William of Durham, who had supported the cause of Robert Curthose.

Bishop William argued that no bishop could be placed on trial in a secular court but must instead be referred to an ecclesiastical council, where he could expect lenient treatment. Lanfranc, for his part, argued that although he was undoubtedly a bishop, he had committed crimes in his capacity as a secular lord who held lands from the king and as such he could be tried by a royal court.

Some of this subtlety may have been lost on William Rufus, who was probably more interested in securing Durham castle before his invasion of Normandy, but Bishop William raised the stakes substantially when he decided to appeal to the court of the pope himself and went into temporary exile.

William Rufus did not share his father's piety. In fact, unusually for this period, he seems not to have cared in the slightest what the church thought of him. He may also have been homosexual.

While Rufus may not have cared much for the teachings of the church, however, he cared a good deal for its money. When abbots died, he simply left their posts empty so as to exploit the royal right of collecting their revenues during vacancies. When Lanfranc died in 1089, Rufus declined to appoint a successor, leaving England's highest ecclesiastical office vacant until 1093!

At Easter in 1093, William Rufus became dangerously ill and was expected to die. Discovering a sudden interest in the state of his soul, he sought to rescue it by making sure that the archbishopric of Canterbury was finally filled. Fortunately, Anselm, the famous Abbot of Bec, had come to court.

Anselm was a former pupil of Lanfranc and regarded as one of the best theologians in the west; his thought continues to influence Christian theology today. He did not want the job and was carried forcefully into church for his consecration. On this occasion, Rufus seems to have been more in tune with the wishes of the divine than Anselm himself, for his health immediately began to recover.

Anselm had considerable respect for the royal office, but his support for William Rufus was far less total than Lanfranc's had been for William the Conqueror. When he could not persuade Rufus to recognise Pope Urban II, he circumvented the king by writing in secret to Urban to ask that his "*Pallium*" (a key symbol of his office) be sent to him.

Rufus's demands for knights and money from Anselm, and his refusal to allow him to convene a church council, drove the archbishop to despair and he eventually went into voluntary exile to seek the pope's advice. He was still in exile when Rufus died. Crucially, Anselm was present at the Council of Rome (Easter 1099), which excommunicated all clergy who received "investiture" of their ecclesiastical office from laymen, or who performed homage to laymen for the lands of their churches.

Anselm returned to England in 1100. The two issues of homage and investiture remained serious points of disagreement between himself and Henry I, but the tone of the debate between the two was civilised, with both parties eager to reach some sort of compromise with each other and with the papacy. Anselm did go into exile again (1103-1106), but a compromise was finally worked out whereby the king would no longer formally nominate bishops or invest them with the symbols of their spiritual office, but could receive their homage for their lands. It was a delightful fudge, and it restored peace between the king and church for decades.

Anselm died in 1109. His two successors, Ralph d'Escures and William of Corbeil, were both able men, but neither was of the calibre of Lanfranc or Anselm, and neither was inclined to reopen the battles over investiture and homage, though they did engage in a long-running argument with the archbishops of York over the relative status of the two archbishoprics (the "Primacy" dispute).

The machinery of the state

Historians of England in this period are often in awe of the extent and sophistication of its apparatus of government. The massive survey of the kingdom's resources known as Domesday Book could not have been achieved by any comparable European monarchy, and was clearly the product of a long and well-developed tradition of administration. That tradition was a tool readily taken up by the Anglo-Norman kings and it placed considerable resources at their command.

That is not to say, however, that the government of England in either the 11th or the 12th century was in any way "modern". The king's government remained deeply personal. As he moved around his domains, so too did the government. Military campaigning required mobility. So did hunting, which absorbed a good deal of his time, and visiting the shrines of saints who protected his realm. Moving around was important, too, in that it enabled the king to make his presence and his power felt.

To some extent, therefore, the royal government can be thought of as the extension of a great, itinerant aristocratic household. As it passed by, with its great panoply of knights, clergy, servants, hangers-on and so forth, it consumed substantial resources.

It is perhaps unsurprising that the names of some of the great offices of the later medieval state are derived from the domestic functions of an aristocratic household. A *constable,* for instance, is literally the officer who looks after the stables.

The financial basis of the medieval state was also entirely different from that of its modern counterparts. The Norman Conquest had introduced the legal idea that all land ultimately belonged to the king and that all others who held land did so only conditionally in exchange for services. And the king himself, of course, was always by far the largest single landowner in the kingdom.

At the time of the Domesday Book, William I held about 18 per cent of all the estates in the kingdom (by value). The extent of the king's "demesne" lands fluctuated constantly. He seized lands from malefactors and received them when aristocratic lines died out. But he also used them as a source of patronage, making gifts to favoured supporters for their loyalty. One of the great tricks of high medieval government was to be generous enough, as king, to retain a wide base of support while not giving away so much as to risk losing financial clout. It was a difficult balancing act that not all kings managed.

In addition to his own lands, the king had the right to many other sources of income. "Feudal aids and Incidents" were rights that kings could exploit on occasion to demand money from his followers for a defined purpose. Payments were made when kings married off their daughters, knighted their sons, or allowed the inheritance of a nobleman to pass to his successor. Payments made by knights to avoid military service ("scutage") eventually became a regular part of taxation.

These rights were all significant sources of revenue, but needed to be exploited with great care. They tended to become customary over the decades, losing their value through inflation. If kings insisted on raising them beyond "traditional" levels, however, they risked facing angry opposition.

Where the royal finances were different from those of the nobility was in the matter of general taxation. The *geld* was part of the Anglo-Saxon inheritance of the English monarchy and remained levied on the hide, usually at a rate of two shillings. This could raise substantial sums (some £2,400 in

1130, for instance). It also ensured that the various landowners were taxed in (very rough) proportion to their ability to pay.

The king had various other means of raising money. Medieval governments tended not to imprison many offenders, preferring to fine them instead, and English monarchs charged litigants for the writs that initiated many legal actions. The king enjoyed the right to the revenues of bishoprics and abbeys after the death of the bishop or abbot until the appointment of his successor.

For the Anglo-Norman kings, justice and the patronage of the church were central to the idea of what monarchy was for, but they were money-spinners, too.

In terms of territorial organisation, William the Conqueror would not allow himself to be trapped as Edward I had been. The title of earl remained in use, but the huge territorial blocks like those that had defined the government of England from Cnut's day were not to re-emerge. William created a series of "Marcher Earldoms" in the west to guard against encroachments by the Welsh and to organise the conquest of parts of Wales where that was practical. The king's main representative in the shires remained the sheriff. Sheriffs might be great aristocrats, and indeed it was possible to hold more than one shrievalty at once, but they were undoubtedly royal servants, collecting the king's taxes, raising his armies, and carrying out the instructions that he sent out by writ.

The reforms of Henry I

In the sphere of domestic administration it is difficult to draw a clear distinction between the achievements of Henry I and those of his formidable ally, Bishop Roger of Salisbury. Roger was deeply involved in the running of Henry's government – especially when the King was in northern France – and seems to have been co-architect of Henry's many reforms.

In contrast to the impious Rufus and the indolent Curthose, Henry won the praise of many contemporaries for his ferocious enforcement of justice, the most dramatic example being the mutilation of the moneyers of England for debasing the coinage.* He reformed the conduct of his itinerant court, forbidding looting by his followers and insisting that the court pay properly for what it consumed. To assist this, members of the court were given fixed subsistence payments.

The most profound of Henry's innovations, however, was the Exchequer – a revolutionary development in financial administration. The heart of the Exchequer was a large, chequered table-cloth used as an abacus, but the word was swiftly applied to the government department that grew up around

---

* In 1124 Henry found that the English penny was not commanding its face value in the market place as a result of this practice. His response was to castrate and remove the right hand from the kingdom's moneyers. The *Anglo-Saxon Chronicle* recounts this story with approval for the king's stern approach to justice.

it. Equipped with expert staff, detailed accounting procedures and its own archive of receipts and expenditures, the Exchequer remained the basis of financial administration throughout the medieval period and gives its name to the modern British finance minister.

Was there a "Norman Empire"?

Writers in the 11th and 12th centuries had a developed language of national identity which they could use to talk about history and government. But though the words "Anglia" and "Normannia" (England and Normandy) had long been in circulation, no word existed that meant "all the lands ruled by the man who is both duke of Normandy and king of England".

In legal terms, there was no question at all that the titles king and duke had different origins. Neither William nor any of his children claimed to rule in Normandy as a king. In practice, of course, the king-duke dealt with English business while in Normandy and with Norman business when in England. His policy was often concerned with the political and military arena of northern France, but he pursued his aims there with treasure and soldiers from England. All this invites the question of whether we should consider England and Normandy to have been a single political unit.

"The Norman Empire" (1976) is the title of a

significant book by Jean Le Patourel.* His thesis was more provisional than the bold title suggests, but it is possible to amass evidence for the cross-Channel integration of England and Normandy after 1066 and for that integration having an "imperial" character (i.e. the subordination of the resources and interests of one people to another). In rewarding his followers with lands in England, the Conqueror created a class of nobility who had a strong interest in maintaining the unity of the two territories under a single ruler. Norman religious houses acquired lands and dependent priories in England (though, notably, the reverse was not true) and a new aristocracy was imposed made up mostly of men of Norman origin or from other parts of northern France.

That said, Le Patourel's argument was already under attack by the late 1980s.** The cross-Channel aristocracy was never very numerous, and began unravelling as soon as it was created: noble families tended to divide their estates among their sons, just as William the Conqueror had done. There was never any question of merging the ecclesiastical administration to extend the authority of the

---

*   J. Le Patourel, *The Norman Empire* (1976)
**   D. Bates, "Normandy and England after 1066", *English Historical Review* 104 (1989), 851-880. Bates has recently returned to this subject in *The Normans and Empire* (2015), though examining the subject on a somewhat different basis, using in particular the ideas of "hard" and "soft" power to argue that England and Normandy were strongly enough linked together to justify the term.

archbishop of Rouen into England. When the Exchequer developed, a parallel institution was created in Normandy. Even if the new "Romanesque" building style was a major departure from pre-1066 architecture in England, it retained English influences. In short, while the Norman Conquest brought into existence a single political world, with a mobile centre in the person and court of the king-duke, the term "Empire" probably creates more problems than it solves.

The reign of King Stephen (1135-1154)

A short summary of Stephen's reign

However impressive his achievements in life, Henry I could not direct events from the grave. Although he had successfully extracted promises of support from his magnates for Maud's accession to the throne, she was not the only grandchild of William the Conqueror available in 1135. Stephen, Count of Mortain, son of the Count of Blois and of Adela, William the Conqueror's daughter, was one of the richest men in the Anglo-Norman world. He was also in Boulogne and could reach England more quickly than Maud.

Aside from his gender, Stephen had a major advantage over "the Empress": the support of his wealthy and powerful brother, Henry of Blois, Bishop of Winchester. It was Henry who persuaded Archbishop William of Canterbury to crown Stephen as king. Bishop Roger of Salisbury, Henry I's great minister, also gave his support. As keen to hold England and Normandy together as they had been in 1088, the Norman nobility soon defected to the new king.

Stephen's embryonic regime ran into problems almost immediately. King David I of Scotland, Maud's uncle, saw an opportunity both to extend his kingdom and to support his niece. He launched an invasion of northern England and occupied Cumberland and Northumberland. Stephen marched north and arranged peace with the Scots at Durham. In mid 1136, a major Welsh rebellion erupted. In 1137, the king was in Normandy where he sought to end Angevin incursions into the duchy, but was unable to deal a serious blow.

His position continued to deteriorate in 1138. David launched further invasions of the north, only contained by Thurstan, Archbishop of York, who organised a desperate defence, but though the northerners won a major victory at Northallerton in the "Battle of the Standard", David could not be dislodged. In April 1139, Stephen effectively accepted defeat in the north by making David's son, Henry, Earl of Northumbria.

Though nominally still subject to the English crown, in practice a great swathe of the north of England was now under Scottish control.

Meanwhile, Robert of Gloucester, an illegitimate son of Henry I and one of the most powerful nobles in England, declared his support for Maud, sparking a series of uprisings against the king across his extensive lands in the west of England. By the end of the year the Welsh rebels had been defeated and the various other threats to Stephen's rule had been contained, but only just.

If 1138 had been difficult, 1139 was calamitous. Believing that Roger of Salisbury himself and his two nephews, Bishop Nigel of Ely and Bishop Alexander of Lincoln, were about to defect to Maud's cause, Stephen tried to arrest the bishops and seize their castles.

This appallingly clumsy move not only guaranteed the outright rebellion of Nigel, who escaped the King's clutches, it also alienated Stephen's most powerful supporter, Henry of Blois, who could not accept that bishops should be subject to secular justice in such an arbitrary fashion. In September, Robert of Gloucester and Maud began an outright invasion of England. The conflict had become a full-blown civil war.

Stephen continued to blunder. In 1140, his army surrounded Maud at Arundel, but he allowed her passage to join up with Robert in the west. In January 1141 he decided to oust Earl Ranulf of Chester from Lincoln castle – a castle which Ranulf had only just been granted – and laid siege to it. He was caught there by a much larger army led by Robert of Gloucester, defeated and captured.

Immediately after the Battle of Lincoln, Stephen's cause must have seemed utterly lost. Henry of Blois defected to Maud and she began to make preparations for an occupation of London and a coronation. Remarkably, Maud managed to bungle the aftermath by refusing to respect the privileges of the increasingly wealthy and powerful city of London.

The Londoners revolted, driving her out. Henry rediscovered his passion for his brother's cause, and his forces fought Maud's in Winchester while the army of Stephen's wife, Matilda, now swollen with the addition of outraged Londoners, closed in. The Empress was defeated and she and David I only just escaped from Winchester. Robert, however, did not. On 1st November 1141, Stephen was released from captivity in exchange for Robert.

Stephen's release prevented the possibility of outright victory for the Angevins. It did not, however, restore order. The next several years were a protracted period of siege warfare and local disorder as nobles exploited the power vacuum to settle old scores and resurrect old claims through low-level local feuding rather than through appeal to the king-duke's justice.

In 1143-4, Count Geoffrey of Anjou completed the conquest of Normandy. The king's reach was now confined to a small portion of southern and eastern England, but he campaigned furiously and hung on.

In 1151, Geoffrey of Anjou died. He had already

made his (and Maud's) son, Henry, Duke of Normandy. Now Henry succeeded to the County of Anjou as well. In 1152 he married the immensely wealthy and powerful Eleanor of Aquitaine. The match made Henry into by far the most powerful man in France, hugely overshadowing King Louis VII. It also equipped him with the resources to launch a new invasion of England.

The stage was set for yet another round of campaigning, but Stephen's heir, Eustace, died in August 1153 and that last blow seems to have finally broken Stephen's will to resist. In November 1153, Stephen and Henry agreed the Treaty of Winchester. Stephen recognised Henry as his heir in exchange for being allowed to remain king for the remainder of his life and for Stephen's surviving son, William, to retain his family lands in Normandy and England. Henry did not have long to wait. Stephen died on 25th October 1154 and Henry II was consecrated king on 19th December.

Was there an "anarchy" in King Stephen's Reign?

The label "anarchy" or even "the Anarchy" took hold in the 19th century among scholars who saw a profound break in the historical development of England in this period. The view was forcefully advanced by J.H. Round, who saw in Stephen's reign an eruption of the English nobility, usually held in check by the power of the crown.[*] His thesis draws some support from the dramatic statements of contemporary chroniclers, who describe the disorders of the reign in almost apocalyptic tones.

Round's argument won wide support in the early 20th century. In a classic article in 1903, "The Anarchy of King Stephen's Reign", H.W.C Davis used the taxation records of the next reign to show that England had suffered a massive loss of taxable wealth that could only be the result of great destruction in the countryside, even if this destruction was localised in character.[**]

Since then, however, other scholars have been chipping away at the "Anarchy" thesis. Modern historians point out that the evidence is unevenly distributed – a disproportionate number of the chroniclers who wrote dramatic descriptions of disorder were based in some of the worst areas of fighting. The king was clearly able to raise enough money to pay his armies. Furthermore, some historians have suggested that government as such did not cease. Instead, it was operated by Robert of Gloucester in the west, David I in the north, and Stephen in the south and east, or at a more local level by other nobles. A great many nobles sought to maintain local peace and stability by making agreements with one another not to participate in

[*]   J.H. Round, *Geoffrey de Mandeville: A study of the Anarchy* (1892)
[**]   H.W.C Davis, "The Anarchy of King Stephen's Reign" *English Historical Review* 18 (1903), 630-641

the fighting. Among the historians who take this less dramatic view is Stephen's biographer, K. Stringer, who advances perhaps the most positive interpretation of his reign.*

The word "anarchy" literally means "the absence of government". The formal processes of government were not literally absent from England during Stephen's reign, but they were certainly weaker and more limited in reach than at any period since at least Aethelred II's reign. If one regards the *purpose* of medieval government as the maintenance of peace and the *effective enforcement* of the king-duke's will then the word anarchy may be justified.

There is one other basis for viewing the collapse of order as particularly severe during Stephen's reign. It seems to have been accompanied by a collapse in the *spiritual* authority of England's higher clergy. They were abused, their churches were often converted into castles for local campaigning, and their excommunications were ignored. The oft-quoted passage in the *Anglo-Saxon Chronicle* that describes the period as one where men "said openly that Christ and his Saints slept" is more specific than is often recognised. It referred not to general disorder but to the apparent ineffectiveness of spiritual authority. In short, the formal processes of government continued, but the king's primary role as the guarantor of peace was not carried out and the

* K. Stringer, *The Reign of Stephen: Kingship, Warfare and Government in Twelfth-Century England* (1993)

disorder affected religious as much as temporal authority. Whether one finds the term "anarchy" useful or not, Stephen's reign was a catastrophe.

Henry II, Thomas Becket and the "Angevin Empire"

A short outline

A whole generation had grown up in the chaos of civil war. It is hardly surprising that there was little domestic opposition to the rule of Henry II. The new king appointed as his chancellor one of the negotiators of the treaty of Winchester, a protégé of Archbishop Theobald of Canterbury called Thomas Becket, a brilliant, eloquent and theatrical man who quickly became a close confidant of the king.

Henry's main early challenges were in his continental lands. Geoffrey of Anjou's will had provided that Henry's younger brother, Geoffrey ("fitz Count") would receive Anjou, the Touraine and Maine, but Henry resisted the implementation of the will. By the summer of 1156, he had seen off Geoffrey's challenge and instead installed his brother as count of Nantes, projecting Angevin power into Brittany. In 1158, Henry conquered the county of Toulouse, where Thomas played a key role. Henry's domains now extended from the Scottish border to the Mediterranean.

In 1161 Archbishop Theobald died and Henry chose Thomas as his replacement. There were few spiritual arguments for the appointment, but a pliant archbishop would be a great advantage in Henry's diplomatic schemes, and by combining the offices of archbishop and chancellor, Henry could imitate the only European ruler with greater power and prestige than his own, Frederick Barbarossa. The monks of Canterbury were persuaded to elect Thomas. He was consecrated archbishop in 1162, having only been ordained priest the day before.

If Henry had expected Becket to be a second Lanfranc, he was sorely mistaken. The new archbishop chose Anselm as his model, but Thomas and Henry II lacked the flexibility and the instinct for compromise of Anselm and Henry I.

Thomas resigned the chancellorship. By 1163, the relationship between king and archbishop was in steep decline. Thomas resisted Henry's policy of converting Sheriff's Aid into crown revenue, much to Henry's anger. Henry put pressure on the bishops to confirm the "traditional" rights of the crown over the church but Thomas resisted. Henry responded by stripping him of the castles and baronies of Berkhamstead and Hythe. Thomas blocked the proposed marriage of Henry's youngest brother William.

Unfortunately for both parties, what had begun as squabbles over individual points of policy soon began to turn into something more fundamental. At Clarendon, Henry placed enormous pressure on

Thomas and the rest of the bishops to accept a written statement of "traditional" customs, the "Constitutions of Clarendon" which clarified some major points of jurisdiction in favour of the secular power. In particular, magnates were not to be excommunicated without royal approval, clergy could not appeal to the pope's court without royal approval, and clergy convicted of crimes were to be handed over to secular courts for punishment. Thomas buckled.

Henry seems to have decided that defeat was not enough for Thomas. He had also to be broken and humiliated. At Northampton in late 1164, he was subjected to a show trial for a series of supposed crimes committed during his tenure as chancellor. Thomas fled, first to Flanders and then to France.

The archbishop spent the next half decade in exile, a period of intense diplomatic activity during which he expanded his knowledge of canon law and caused considerable annoyance to Pope Alexander III, who was more concerned with his own struggles against Barbarossa than he was with Thomas's dispute with Henry. The two were formally reconciled in 1170 and Thomas returned to England, but little was done on the king's side to implement the terms of their agreement. Henry's officers treated Thomas with open disrespect and the archbishop excommunicated all his English "enemies". Henry was enraged. Seeing his explosion of anger, a group of four of the king's knights rode to Canterbury, where on 29th December they

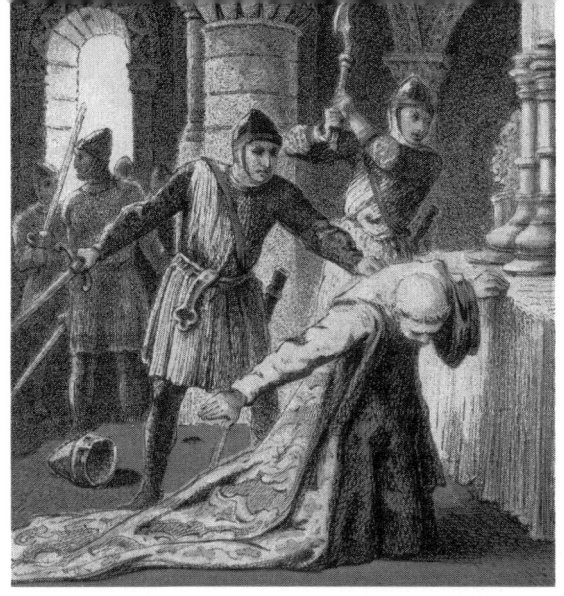

An illustration of the murder of Thomas Becket in 1170

confronted Thomas in Canterbury Cathedral and murdered him.

Acrimonious debates about jurisdiction were one thing. Murdering an archbishop in his own cathedral was something quite different. Public opinion across Europe was shocked by the murder. Henry's French lands and then Henry himself were laid under interdict. In 1172, Henry made elaborate penance for Thomas's murder and even agreed to go on crusade. Thomas's dramatic death had already begun the formation of a saint's cult, a cult which Henry and his family could only neutralise by becoming its adherents.

Not all eyes, however, were fixed on Canterbury. Henry had secured papal licence to conduct an invasion of Ireland as early as the 1150s, but his hand was forced by the ambitions of an Anglo-Norman aristocrat, Richard Fitz Gilbert ("Strongbow") de Clare. Strongbow launched an invasion of Ireland in 1169-70 in support of the ambitions of the king of Leinster, Dermot Mac Murrough. When Dermot died in 1171, Strongbow found himself ruler of much of Ireland. Henry's nobles could not be allowed to become kings with independent power bases abroad. Henry crossed to Ireland with an army to assert his overlordship and forestall that eventuality. It is a striking demonstration of his power that, even when distracted by the aftermath of the Becket dispute, he ended up lord of yet another nation almost by accident.

Even at the peak of his power, however, Henry II was not invulnerable. He had concocted an elaborate scheme for dividing his huge lands among his children at his death, but his eldest son Henry ("the Young King") who had been crowned in his father's lifetime to ensure a smooth succession, chafed against the authority of an overbearing father who would not delegate real power, much as Robert Curthose had chafed against his father a century before.

When Henry II decided to give away some of the Young King's castles to his youngest brother, John, the tension between father and son erupted into outright war. The revolt of 1173-74 saw the Young King, his brother Richard (the future Richard the Lionheart), Eleanor of Aquitaine and King William the Lion of Scotland all ranged against Henry II. All, however, were defeated and the humiliating Treaty of Falaise was imposed on Scotland, decisively breaking Scottish power for the remainder of Henry's reign.

Tensions between the elder and the younger Henrys exploded again in 1182-3, but the Young King died before they could develop into a more general war. In 1186, matters grew worse when Richard, fearing that Henry would make John his principal heir, allied with King Philip II of France and launched yet another rebellion. By now Henry was an old man, and no longer a match for the ruthless young Richard and his allies. He was losing the war when on 5th July 1189 he received the shattering news that John too had joined the rebellion. Henry died the next day.

The restoration of the English state

The England that Henry II inherited from Stephen was a shambles, but he set about the task of reconstruction with enormous energy and skill. There was a contradiction at the heart of his government – on the one hand, his rule was self-consciously nostalgic, looking back constantly to the rule of Henry I for inspiration and legitimacy. (Stephen's reign he regarded as an interregnum.) On the other hand, Henry was an innovator who drove the development of the English state apparatus far beyond what his grandfather had achieved.

As early as 1155, Henry ordered the return of all the royal lands that had been given away or otherwise lost under Stephen. He dismissed the great majority of Stephen's sheriffs. He set about the demolition of the unauthorised castles that had sprung up and installed Bishop Nigel of Ely to take over his uncle's old role of running the Exchequer, which was gradually brought back into full working order. The royal monopoly over the coinage was restored and in 1158 the coinage was reissued.

For all his other achievements, it is in the field of law that Henry's reputation is highest among English historians. He has traditionally been credited with the foundation of a truly national system of justice known as the English "Common Law". Henry I's system of "Justices in Eyre" – teams of judges who travelled on "circuits" around the kingdom hearing cases and judging them by a national standard – was reinvigorated and extended. In particular, by making them responsible for overseeing the implementation of "assizes" (formal statements modifying custom which have been considered the forerunners of Acts of Parliament), Henry made the Justices in Eyre into the linchpin of the judicial system.

In so doing, the role of the sheriff was reduced and a great step forward taken in the centralisation of the realm. At the same time, the role of juries in trials and inquests was greatly expanded. Juries had been used by earlier monarchs to provide a local view of technical matters like the ownership of property, but under Henry they became a key component of the system, largely replacing the early medieval practice of trial by combat.

What was the Becket Crisis really about?

There are a number of possible ways to answer this question.

1. A clash of personalities
It is possible to read the Becket Crisis as a personal clash between Henry Plantagenet and Thomas Becket. It is a striking fact that however great the shock at Thomas's murder, his episcopal colleagues did not choose to share his exile. His most trenchant critic was another bishop (and indeed a monk and theologian), Gilbert Foliot.

Henry was outraged at his apparent betrayal by a close friend, a man, moreover, of obscure background whom Henry himself had elevated to high office. Thomas's theatrical behaviour and the king's inflexibility and implacable anger caused a series of serious but manageable disagreements to spiral out of control.

This interpretation has been given much support by hagiographies (saints' lives) of Thomas which sought to reconcile knowledge of the chancellor's worldliness with his later reputation as a saint and which did so by emphasising the transformational experience of his elevation to the archbishopric. A clash of personalities between two old friends is easier to explain if one of those personalities has suddenly changed.

2. Church and crown

An alternative reading of events is to see in the contest an expression of the wider tensions between secular and ecclesiastical authority produced by Papal Reform. After all, Thomas was not the first archbishop of Canterbury driven to exile by his arguments with an English king.

As has been seen, some of Henry's most important work concerned the extension, systematisation and clarification of the law. Compromise on the part of prelates with jurisdictional demands made by the secular power grew more difficult as canon law grew more elaborate and more clearly defined. In that sense, the dispute can be seen as a point of collision between two expanding and incompatible legal systems.

3. The rights of Canterbury

In contrast to either the grandiose or the personal, it is possible to see Thomas as an archbishop *of Canterbury* above all else. One recent account, by Henry Mayr-Harting, lays heavy emphasis on this approach, arguing that whatever other issues were subsequently drawn into the conflict it began when Thomas tried to recover some of Canterbury's estates from associates of the king who were not minded to return them, and that this poisoned the relationship between Thomas and Henry beyond recovery.[*]

These different schools of thought need not, of course, be considered mutually exclusive. Nor must we assume that the protagonists' ideas remained fixed throughout. The dispute went on for years and Thomas certainly seems to have conceived the struggle in increasingly grand terms over time. In particular, it it difficult to disentangle the idea of "personality" from the theatrical performance that was so essential to medieval politics and equally difficult to disentangle Thomas's idea of Canterbury from his idea of the wider church.

Conclusion

The England of 1189 was a very different place from the England of 1035. It was more populous, richer, and more technologically sophisticated. A visitor from one period dropped into the other would be struck powerfully by changes in everything from architecture to language. Contemporaries were well aware that they lived in a period of major political upheaval, but they also felt a powerful sense of connection to the past. Indeed, the period after the Norman Conquest saw a great flowering of written history in England.

[*]   H. Mayr-Harting, *Religion, Politics and Society in Britain 1066-1272* (2011)

When Thomas Becket lay dying in Canterbury Cathedral, he called out for the intercession of one of his predecessors, Aelfheah, the Anglo-Saxon archbishop murdered by the Danes in 1016. In the picture of two archbishops of Canterbury cut down by warriors for failing to comply with the demands of secular power, it is difficult not to see something of deep continuity. At least four strands of that continuity must always be borne in mind.

1. Europe

For almost the whole of this period, the king of England was also the ruler of major territories outside it, first in Scandinavia, later in France. The king of England was not merely *sometimes* on the continent. He was *usually* on the continent. Holding, protecting and, when possible, expanding his continental lands was always a key priority, and no history of the English monarchy in this period is even remotely convincing without a good deal of attention paid to the turbulent politics of France.

The English church, moreover, was one arm of a vast international organisation with its centre in Rome which from the mid 11th-century was engaged in a series of battles to transform itself and the rest of the Christian world in its own image. Those battles could take the form of polite legal debate, show trials or even crusades, but their impact was felt throughout the Christian world, and England was no exception.

2. State power

Whatever the material and cultural damage done by the Danish and Norman Conquests, the conquerors always understood that in the English state apparatus they had an instrument of unusual power and potential, not one to be cast aside lightly. The very fact that English kings were so often absent from the kingdom required the development of ever more elaborate mechanisms of government so that the king's business could continue even if the man himself was elsewhere.

3. Succession crises

Sophisticated means of raising revenue and armies, and of administering justice, were no protection from dynastic instability. Any system of government that depends on heredity is subject to profound shocks when family squabbles are magnified through the lens of high politics and the resources of the state, transforming the failure to produce heirs of the right age, gender or personality at the right time from a family problem into a national or even international calamity.

It is often pointed out that a general transformation in inheritance practice across the west occurred in the late 11th and early 12th century, with primogeniture gradually displacing other models of inheritance. That is generally so, but it it worth remembering that in this entire period the crown *never* passed peacefully from the king to his eldest son.

4. Luck

However conscious we are of the personalities and the structural factors that drive historical change, the effect of sheer chance is a key force that must not be forgotten, a force magnified by the inherent instability of dynastic politics and the dangers of battle.

Had Edward the Confessor lived another five years, had the weather been different in the summer and autumn of 1066, had William rather than Harold been killed at Hastings, had the White Ship made it safely into port, the history of the entire period would certainly have looked very different.

FURTHER READING

General

The best introductory book on England in the period is R. Bartlett, *England under the Norman and Angevin Kings 1075-1225* (2000). For a more British Approach, D. Carpenter, *The Struggle for Mastery: Britain 1066-1284* (2003)

The kings

Yale publishes the standard biographies in this period in their *English Monarchs* series. Particularly important are F. Barlow, *Edward the Confessor* (1970), D.C. Douglas *William the Conqueror: The Norman Impact Upon England* (1964), C.W Hollsiter, *Henry I* (2001) and Edmund King, *King Stephen* (2010).

See also D. Bates, *William the Conqueror* (1989). A very significant book for understanding many of the issues of William's reign, though this is shorter and less detailed than Douglas" book and should be read alongside it.

Economic history

C. Dyer, *Making a Living in the Middle Ages: The People of Britain, 850-1520* (2002)

Women's history

H. Leyser, *Medieval Women: A Social History of Women in England, 450-1500* (1988)

The church

H. Mayr-Harting, *Religion, Politics and Society in Britain, 1066-1272* (2011)

England and Europe

Essays in (eds.) M. Jones, M. Vale, *England and Her Neighbours 1066-1453: Essays in Honour of Pierre Chaplais* (1989)

For the wider context and for many of the key ideas informing how historians think about this period, R. Bartlett, *The Making of Europe: Conquest, Colonization and Cultural Change (1993)* is essential.

ⅭⅭ CONNELL GUIDES

MORE IN OUR NEW HISTORY SERIES

Guides
The French Revolution
Winston Churchil
World War One
The Third Reich
Stalin
Lenin
Nelson
The Tudors
Napoleon
The Cold War
The American Civil Rights

Movement
The Normans
Russia and its Rulers

Short Guides
Britain after World War Two
Edward VI
Mary I
The General Strike
The Suffragettes
President Truman
President Lincoln

"Connell Guides should be required reading in every school in the country."
Julian Fellowes, creator of Downton Abbey

"What Connell Guides do is bring immediacy and clarity: brevity with depth. They unlock the complex and offer students an entry route."
Colin Hall, Head of Holland Park School

"These guides are a godsend. I'm so glad I found them."
Jessica Enthoven, A Level student, St Mary's Calne

"Completely brilliant. I wish I were young again with these by my side. It's like being in a room with marvellous tutors. You can't really afford to be without them, and they are a joy to read."
Joanna Lumley

To buy any of these guides, or for more information, go to
www.connellguides.com
Or contact us on (020)79932644 / info@connellguides.com

LITERATURE GUIDES

Novels and poetry
Emma
Far From the Madding Crowd
Frankenstein
Great Expectations
Hard Times
Heart of Darkness
Jane Eyre
Lord of the Flies
Mansfield Park
Middlemarch
Mrs Dalloway
Paradise Lost
Persuasion
Pride and Prejudice
Tess of the D'Urbervilles
The Canterbury Tales
The Great Gatsby
The Poetry of Robert Browning
The Waste Land
To Kill A Mockingbird
Wuthering Heights

Shakespeare
A Midsummer Night's Dream
Antony and Cleopatra
Hamlet
Julius Caesar

King Lear
Macbeth
Othello
Romeo and Juliet
The Second Tetralogy
The Tempest
Twelfth Night

Modern texts
A Doll's House
A Room with a View
A Streetcar Named Desire
An Inspector Calls
Animal Farm
Atonement
Beloved
Birdsong
Hullabaloo
Never Let Me Go
Of Mice and Men
Rebecca
Spies
The Bloody Chamber
The Catcher in the Rye
The History Boys
The Road
Vernon God Little
Waiting for Godot

NEW
A Short History of English
Literature
American literature
Dystopian literature

How to read a poem
How to read Shakespeare
The Gothic
The poetry of Christina Rossetti
Women in literature

For my father and mother, who took me to castles and cathedrals.

First published in 2017 by
Connell Guides
Spye Arch House
Spye Park
Lacock
Wiltshire
SN15 2PR

10 9 8 7 6 5 4 3 2 1

A CIP catalogue record for this book is available from the British Library.
ISBN 978-1-911187-71-4

Design © Nathan Burton

Assistant Editors and typeset by:
Brian Scrivener and Paul Woodward

Printed in Great Britain

www.connellguides.com